D1237872

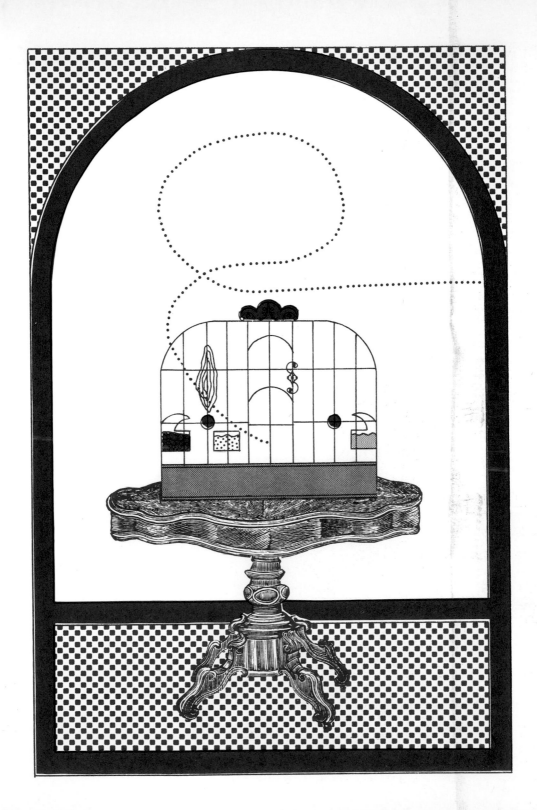

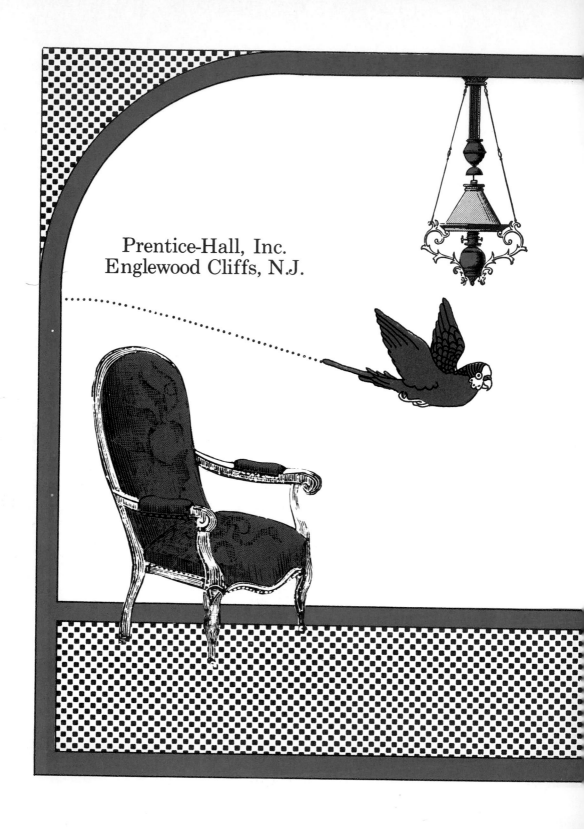

Prentice-Hall, Inc.
Englewood Cliffs, N.J.

SALVADOR
AND
MISTER SAM

A GUIDE TO PARAKEET CARE

By Gail Gibbons

BELMONT COLLEGE LIBRARY

To the Poodge

78563

Copyright © 1975 by Gail Gibbons

All rights reserved. No part of this book may be
reproduced in any form or by any means, except
for the inclusion of brief quotations in a review,
without permission in writing from the publisher.

Printed in the United States of America ·J

Prentice-Hall International, Inc., London
Prentice-Hall of Australia, Pty. Ltd., North Sydney
Prentice-Hall of Canada, Ltd., Toronto
Prentice-Hall of India, Private Ltd., New Delhi
Prentice-Hall of Japan, Inc., Tokyo

Library of Congress Cataloging in Publication Data

Gibbons, Gail.
   Salvador and Mr. Sam: a guide to caring for your
parakeet.

   SUMMARY: Describes how a boy and girl each
care for their pet parakeet from birth to adulthood.
   1. Budgerigars—Juvenile literature.
[1. Budgerigars. 2. Birds] I. Title.
SF473.B8G5   636.6'864   75-11530
ISBN 0-13-788224-6

JUV
PZ
473

B8
G5

Howdy! I'm Sonia.
I'm going to tell you about what fun I've had learning
from my pet parakeet, Mister Sam, and my friend,
Salvador.

Salvador has two pet parakeets, one named Sidney and one named Sue. Sidney has a blue nose because he is a boy, and Sue has a brown nose because she is a girl. The nose of a parakeet is called a cere.

When he first got them, Salvador watched Sue and
Sidney very carefully. The parakeets chased each other
around, bobbed their heads up and down at each other,
and made quiet kissing sounds. Sidney even fed Sue
seeds from his mouth. Soon they were a year old,
old enough to have babies.

At that time, Salvador attached a nest box to their cage.
In a week Sue was spending more and more time in the
nest box. Salvador knew not to disturb them, only to
give them fresh food and water. They needed quiet.
Sue laid one egg every other day until there were five
beautiful eggs in the nest box.
And she stayed nestled right on top of them.

About eighteen days after each egg was laid, a little baby parakeet was hatched from each one. I went to see them, and Salvador promised me a baby bird when they were able to leave their parents. I thought they were pink and ugly! But Salvador was proud of the clutch.
A clutch is a group of baby birds.

We're rare indeed!

The clutch was rare indeed!
Usually parakeets only have babies when they are in a
group of parakeets. Most of the time they are paired off
into separate cages but still should be able to see and
hear the other birds. Sue and Sidney had had their
babies by themselves with no other birds around.

The next time I visited, the babies had beautiful feathers. They were six weeks old, old enough to leave the clutch. And my mother had said I could pick a baby bird to bring home for my very own.

Salvador bragged to me about all of the tricks he had
taught Sidney and Sue. Sidney flew to his finger...
Sue punched her toy penguin...
Sidney climbed a ladder...
Sue would put her head under her bell.
She looked ridiculous.

And I found that a parakeet could possibly learn to talk!
Salvador said it took a lot of time and patience, but if a
word or phrase was repeated slowly and precisely to a
bird, the bird would learn to speak. He said the voice
would sound scratchy and not like a human voice.
But poor Salvador tried and tried, and Sue and Sidney
still didn't talk.

We went to the pet shop with a list of bird supplies
Salvador had made for me. What a pile of cages!
We picked a sturdy cage that would give my bird enough
room to move and fly around. "The bigger, the better,"
Salvador said. The cage we picked had a water cup, seed
cups and four perches in it. We bought gravel paper for
the bottom of the cage. Salvador said not to put
newspaper in the bottom of the cage because parakeets
love to tear up paper. Also the ink could make
my bird sick.

We needed gravel. Parakeets don't have teeth so they need gravel to break up the seed to digest it. We bought a cuttlebone to supply my little bird with calcium and to keep his beak sharp.

We bought mixed bird seed for parakeets, which consists of millet seed, oats, canary seed and salt. For variety, we also bought Treat food, which contains a larger mixture of seeds. Treat is made up of millet, canary seed, oats, flax, thistle, sesame, bird biscuit, and egg flakes.

There were so many bird toys to choose from!
I was careful not to pick any toys that were sharp or
pointed. I also avoided toys with string because my pet
could easily get tangled in it. So, I bought a mirror,
a roly-poly man, a bell, and a swing.

Parakeets first came from Australia where they're called budgies. You can tell how old your parakeet is by looking at the feather lines on the head. As the bird gets older, the lines will go away, and a solid color will appear just above the cere. Salvador said not to be frightened when your bird loses feathers now and then. He will only be moulting. Moulting is the way birds get rid of their old feathers to grow new ones.

Parakeets only grow to be six inches long. They are
many different colors - blue, yellow, green, even white.
A white parakeet is called an albino. Salvador had
heard that parakeets should not have more than two
clutches a year or the birds become sickly and tired.
Parakeets usually live to be about seven years old.

When we got back to Salvador's house, I wanted to take my pet home right away. Salvador slowly moved his cupped hand toward the bird I had picked, gently picked him up and put him into the cage. He then covered the cage with a towel to keep the bird and the cage warm on my trip home.

I set up the cage right away to make my parakeet feel right at home. I promised to clean the cage at least three times a week and to give my pet fresh seed and water every day. Occasionally, parakeets like greens, so I would put some lettuce in the cage. I didn't need to worry about my pet overeating, because parakeets don't overeat.

After a few weeks, my parakeet's cere turned blue.
He was a boy!
He needed a name, so Mister Sam he became!
And I talked and talked to him.

When Mister Sam was used to his new home, I took him out of the cage. He loved flying around the room. And I even finger trained him. By gently pushing my finger against his chest, he stepped onto my finger. Mister Sam even learned to sit on my shoulder.

And I talked and talked to him.

At night I covered his cage to prevent drafts from chilling him. Mister Sam slept in such a silly position, on one leg with his head resting on his back.

When Salvador finally came to visit, Mister Sam
surprised him with all of the tricks he had learned.
What a showoff! Salvador didn't know Mister Sam
flew around the house, so when Mister Sam took off...

Finally Mister Sam settled.

Salvador was surprised when Mister Sam stepped
onto my finger but...

he was really surprised when Mister Sam spoke.

Salvador was so happy!
And Mister Sam and I were proud.

BELMONT COLLEGE LIBRARY